Windows 10
Jump Start

Just What You Need to Know to Get Started!

By Bob Roberts

About the Author

Bob Roberts has an extensive background in Windows training, having taught millions through his written words and classroom instruction during the past twenty-plus years. Though Windows users throughout the world have read Bob's work, attended his training seminars and followed his expert advice, this is his first book published as "Bob Roberts." Bob continues to work with Microsoft Corporation on a variety of Windows-related projects, including training courses and documentation.

Table of Contents

1. Introducing Windows 10 & Jump Start

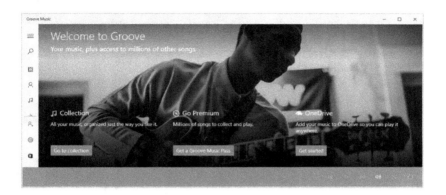

Windows 10 provides an immersive experience unlike any previous release of the operating system. Not only do many new features and advanced options differentiate it from previous releases, but the operating system is designed to run more quickly and efficiently.

When you first start working with Windows 10, you'll notice that it combines many of the best features of Windows 7 and Windows 8.1. From Windows 7, you get many core features and options that users love, including the traditional Start Menu. From Windows 8.1, you get a consistent user interface across mobile and desktop devices.

Windows 10 also has many new features that are exclusive to the operating system and haven't been available previously.

> **TIP**: Throughout this book, where I use click, right-click, and double-click, you can use the touch equivalents of tap, press-and-hold, and double-tap.

Finally, don't forget this book is intended as a quick reference too. Whenever you have a question about any task this book covers, simply open the book, look up the task and follow the step-by-step instructions.

2. Getting to Know Windows 10

Windows 10 is the newest operating system from Microsoft. The operating system is offered as a free upgrade for certain users, including those with:

- Qualified Windows 7 devices
- Qualified Windows 8.1 devices

Windows 10 also comes preinstalled on new devices, including desktops, laptops and tablets. Other users and businesses must purchase Windows 10.

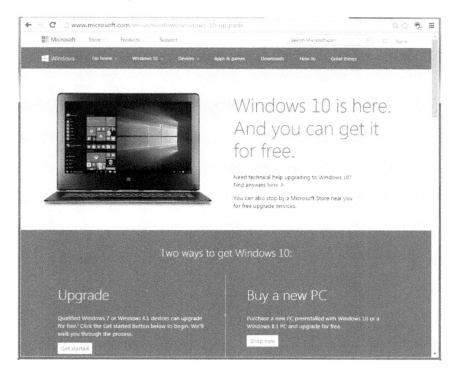

Windows 10 was officially released on July 29, 2015, and is supposedly, the last version of Windows—though it's hard to say whether that's really true or simply a marketing tactic. More likely, it's the last version of Windows that will be delivered as a software product purchased through stores—with future releases of the operating system coming directly from Microsoft.

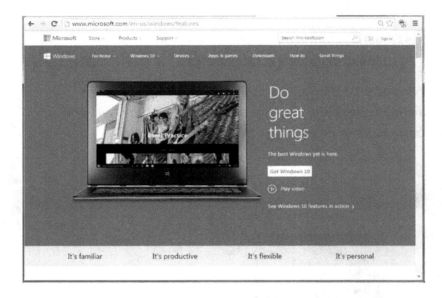

This latest version of Windows is optimized for both touch-screen and the traditional mouse-and-keyboard interfaces. The operating system has many features of both Windows 7 and Windows 8.1 and also brings back the Start Menu, though tablet users may continue to see a Start screen whenever they use Tablet mode.

NOTE: Windows 7, Windows 8 and Windows 8.1 were previous releases of the Windows operating system with Windows 8.1 being an update to the original Windows 8 release. Rather than referring to Windows 8/8.1 throughout this book, I simply refer to Windows 8.1.

If you haven't installed Windows 10 yet, find out if you qualify for a free upgrade by visiting http://www.microsoft.com/en-us/windows/windows-10-upgrade.

The minimum hardware requirements for using Windows 10 are:

- 1 gigahertz (GHz) or faster processor (or a System on a Chip (SoC) device, such as a Windows Phone)
- 1 gigabyte (GB) of RAM for 32-bit systems, 2 GB of RAM for 64-bit systems
- 16 GB of disk space for 32-bit systems, 20 GB of disk space for 64-bit systems
- Graphics card with DirectX 9 or later with WDDM 1.0 or later drivers

New features in Windows 10 include:

- Fast start up that can use Hyperboot and Instant Go to quickly resume
- Microsoft Edge browser for a streamlined web browsing experience
- Cortana, a digital assistant, to help get things done quickly using your voice
- Windows Hello, a security feature that allows login with a look or a touch (on systems with cameras, fingerprint readers and other compliant hardware)
- Virtual Desktop System for creating virtual desktops and seeing open tasks in a single view.
- Continuum which allows you to switch easily and instantly between desktop and tablet mode.

- OneDrive which allows you to easily store documents and photos in the cloud and then access those documents and photos anywhere you can use your account.
- Windows Store for purchasing apps, movies, music, games and more.
- Xbox app for streaming games from your Xbox to your Windows 10 device and staying connected to the Xbox Live community.
- Other new apps like Weather, Photos, Groove Music, Maps, Movies & TV and more.

3. Windows 10 Editions

Like ice cream, Windows 10 comes in different flavors. Each of which is tailored to the needs of different users. You also can compare editions to find the one that's right for you by visiting http://www.microsoft.com/en-us/WindowsForBusiness/Compare.

Windows 10 Home Edition

Windows 10 Home Edition is designed for end-users who use the operating system at home and need only the core essential features. This means you get:

- Continuum
- Cortana
- Microsoft Edge
- Unified settings
- Universal apps
- Virtual Desktop System
- Windows Hello
- More...

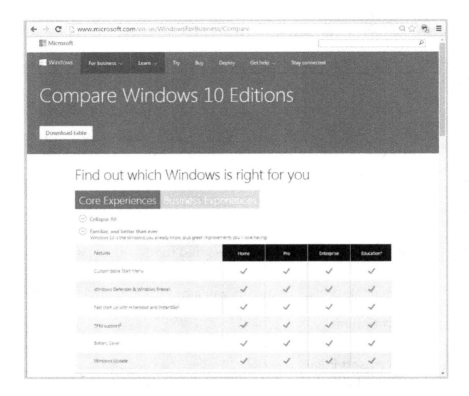

Windows 10 Home Edition replaces Windows 7 Home Basic and Windows 7 Home Premium as well as the basic editions for Windows 8.1. The Home Edition supports a maximum of 4 GB RAM on 32-bit systems and 128 GB RAM on 64-bit systems.

> **TIP**: If you have a Home edition of Windows 7 or Windows 8.1, you must upgrade to Windows 10 Home Edition. You can't upgrade to other editions.

Windows 10 Pro Edition

Windows 10 Pro Edition is designed for professionals who use the operating system at work and need extra features for enhanced security, joining domains and connecting to workplaces. This means you get all the features of the Home Edition plus:

- Assigned Access
- BitLocker Drive Encryption
- Client Hyper-V
- Domain Join & Azure Directory Join
- Enterprise Data Protection
- Group Policy Management
- Remote Desktop
- Windows Store for Business
- Windows Update for Business
- More...

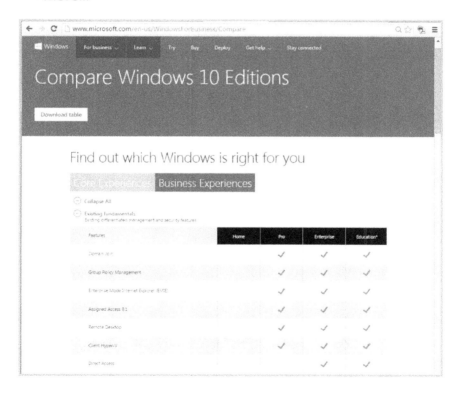

Windows 10 Pro is optimized for those who work in small and medium-sized businesses and can also be used by those who work from home and need to connect to workplaces. Windows 10 Pro replaces Windows 7 Professional and Windows 7 Ultimate as well as the pro editions for Windows 8.1. The Pro Edition supports a maximum of 4 GB RAM on 32-bit systems and 512 GB RAM on 64-bit systems.

> **TIP**: If you have a pro edition of Windows 7 or Windows 8.1, you must upgrade to Windows 10 Pro. You can't upgrade to Windows 10 Home or Enterprise Edition.

Windows 10 Enterprise & Education Editions

Windows 10 Enterprise Edition is designed for professionals who use the operating system in enterprise business settings and large offices. With the Enterprise Edition, you get all the features of Home and Pro plus the extra features needed for deploying and managing Windows 10 on a large scale, including:

- App Locker
- BranchCache
- Direct Access
- Credential Guard
- Device Guard
- Long Term Servicing Branch of Windows 10
- Windows To Go
- More...

Windows 10 Enterprise replaces Windows 7 Enterprise as well as the enterprise edition for Windows 8.1. The Enterprise Edition supports a maximum of 4 GB RAM on 32-bit systems and 512 GB RAM on 64-bit systems.

> **TIP**: If you have an Enterprise edition of Windows 7 or Windows 8.1, you must upgrade to Windows 10 Enterprise Edition. You can't upgrade to the Home or Pro editions.

Windows 10 Education Edition

Windows 10 Education Edition is meant for use by students and those in academia, such as university faculty and professors. This edition has the same features as the Enterprise Edition.

This means you get all the features of Home and Pro plus extra features needed for deploying and managing Windows 10 throughout educational organizations, including:

- App Locker
- BranchCache
- Direct Access
- Credential Guard
- Device Guard
- Windows To Go
- More...

Windows 10 Education replaces Windows 7 Education as well as the education edition for Windows 8.1. The Education Edition supports a maximum of 4 GB RAM on 32-bit systems and 512 GB RAM on 64-bit systems.

> **TIP**: If you have an Education edition of Windows 7 or Windows 8.1, you must upgrade to Windows 10 Education Edition. You can't upgrade to the Home, Pro or Enterprise editions.

Windows 10 Mobile Editions

Windows 10 comes in two mobile versions:

- Windows 10 Mobile Edition
- Windows 10 Mobile Enterprise Edition

Windows 10 Mobile Edition is designed for use on small personal devices that use touch interfaces, such as smartphones and small tablet PCs. The Mobile Edition supports:

- Continuum for Phone
- Touch-optimized Office
- Universal apps
- Unified settings
- More...

Windows 10 Mobile Enterprise Edition is designed for use on small personal devices that are connected to enterprises. Anyone who uses personal smartphones and small tablet PCs at work can use this edition to get enterprise enhancements for security, management and more.

Windows 10 Internet of Things Editions

If you thought the six flavors of Windows 10 was all that was available, think again. Windows 10 is also available in a variety of other editions, including:

- Windows 10 Internet of Things for Industry Devices
- Windows 10 Internet of Things for Mobile Devices
- Windows 10 Internet of Things for Small Devices

These editions are designed for devices used in a variety of home, business and industrial settings and include:

- Desktop Shell for core functionality
- Win32 Apps, Universal Apps and drivers

Although you may find Windows 10 Internet of Things for Small Devices in home appliances and Windows 10 Internet of Things for Mobile Devices in small mobile gadgets and accessories, such as smart watches, you likely won't encounter Windows 10 Internet of Things for Industry Devices unless you work in a light or heavy industry setting.

Windows 10 coffee pot anyone?

4. Getting Virtual Assistance

Personal digital assistants are in vogue. Apple has Siri. Google has Google Now. Microsoft has Cortana.

Cortana is designed to provide help and guidance and can be activated in several different ways:

- Cortana can be made available for any time you search the web or Windows.
- Cortana can be used to give you time- and location-based reminders.
- Cortana can also be used to create appointments, set alerts and more.

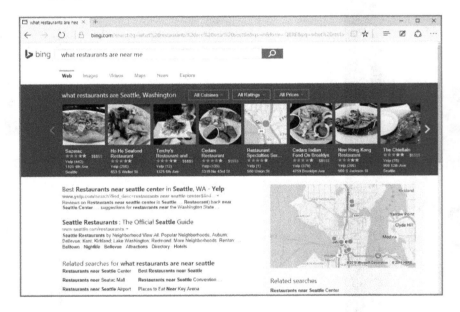

You can ask Cortana questions. For example, you can ask "What restaurants are near me" or "What coffee shops are near me." Cortana will use location information to determine what restaurants or coffee shops are nearby and display information about them. If you say "show my recent photos" or "find my recent word documents," Cortana will search your account for those types of files and display them.

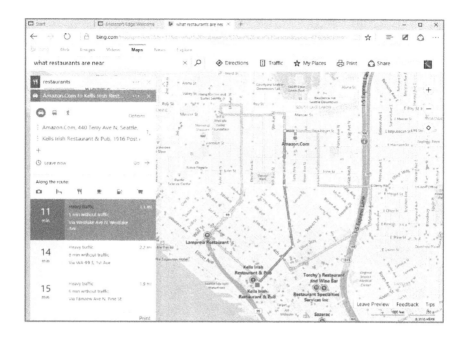

Cortana's natural language abilities are the key to how digital assistance works. As you talk to Cortana, the program learns your voice and gets better at understanding you.

5. A New Browsing Experience

Microsoft Edge replaces Internet Explorer as the default browser in Windows 10. The Edge browser provides a streamlined browsing experience that gets rid of much of the windows frame and interface to let you see more of what you want to see—namely the websites you are visiting.

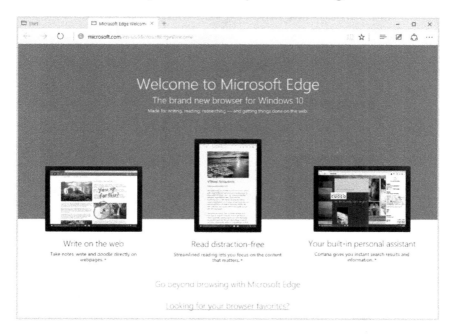

Edge also gets rid of legacy technologies like ActiveX and adds extensions that are more secure and current with the times, including integration with OneDrive and Cortana. Although Edge has many new features, a few that you may use the most are:

- Reading View—A streamlined reading experience that fills the screen and makes it easier to read without distractions.
- Reading List—An enhanced bookmarking feature that lets you save articles or other content that you want to read later.
- Web Note—A notation tool that allows you to take notes, write or doodle directly on web pages and then see those annotations any time you visit the web page.

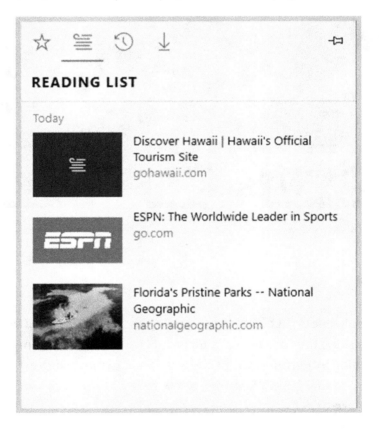

Just because Edge has replaced Internet Explorer as the default browser doesn't mean Internet Explorer isn't available or hasn't been updated. Windows 10 still includes Internet Explorer and the browser can be used for those times when you need access to legacy features such as ActiveX or simply anytime you want to use this popular browser. Internet Explorer version 11, IE 11, is what is available with the original release of Windows 10.

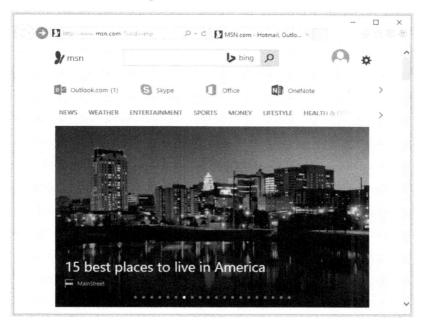

Internet Explorer 11 is an improved version of the original web browser that's been in Windows for many years. Although IE 11 has a streamlined interface similar to Microsoft Edge, IE 11 doesn't have the same features as Edge. With IE 11, you can't write on web pages or get instant search results with Cortana. There isn't a reading list or a Reading View either. That said, as the figure that follows shows, web pages opened in IE 11 will look substantially similar to those opened in Microsoft Edge.

6. Apps on the Go

Universal apps are a key benefit of Windows 10 that you may not be familiar with. As the name implies, universal apps are apps that run across various types of devices seamlessly, from desktops to tablets, smartphones and even Xbox One devices.

Many universal apps are installed on Windows 10 devices out of the box. These apps are available via the Start Menu, as shown in the preceding figure, and include:

- Calendar—a built-in calendar app that allows you to create events and get reminders for appointments.

- Mail—a built-in mail program that you can use to connect and access all your email in one place.
- Microsoft Edge—a web browser with a streamlined interface that allows you to easily add notes to your favorite web pages.
- Photos—a digital collection of all your photos that allows you to create photo albums and share your pictures across devices.
- Weather—a handy weather app that allows you to quickly view the current weather and get weather forecasts
- Groove Music—a music app that puts all your digital music in one place and provides quick access to the music available in the Windows Store.
- Movies & TV—a video player that replaces Windows Media Player and lets you watch movies, television shows and digital videos.
- Maps—a map tool for getting directions and learning about nearby restaurants, stores, coffee houses and more.
- News—a news app for getting local, national and world news.

Many other apps are available for download or purchase in the Windows Store. Anyone familiar with the Google Play or Apple iTunes store knows what the Windows Store is all about.

The Windows Store is where you go to purchase apps, games, music, movies and more. And visiting the Windows Store is as simple as clicking **Store** on the Start Menu.

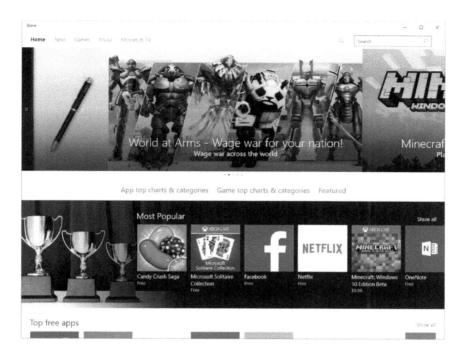

Because store apps are universal apps, any app you use on one device can also be made available on your other devices. Here's how it works:

1. You download or purchase an app in the Windows store using your account.
2. When you sign in to that same account on another device, the app is available for download and install on that device too.
3. If you create files in the app and store the files in OneDrive (the free cloud service for saving files mentioned earlier), those files will be available too.

How cool is that? It's okay, you don't have to answer the question by screaming "Holy sh*t!" out loud (unless you want to).

7. Settings That Go With You

Unified settings are another key benefit of Windows 10 that you may not be familiar with. As the name implies, unified settings allow you to customize certain aspects of the operating system and have those same settings whenever you log in to your account on any device.

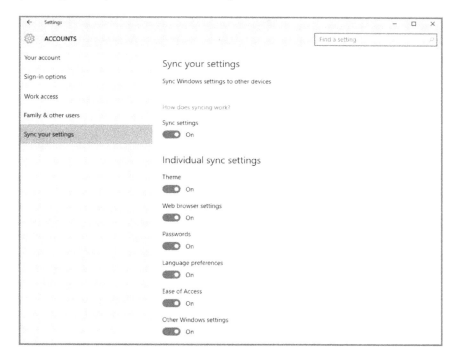

Unified settings rely on the Sync Settings option being enabled, which it is by default. Here's how it works:

1. You log in to your device with your account and personalize Windows and the Edge browser.
2. When you sign in to that same account on another device, the settings are used automatically. This means your favorite colors, account picture, browser favorites and much more will all be there without you having to do anything!

8. Signing In

If you upgraded to Windows 10 from Windows 7, the Windows 10 interface may look a little different than you're used to—and that's because a lot has changed. To avoid getting confused as you try to find your way around, you need to take a few moments to learn where things are in the new Windows. You also need to learn about the new Start menu (or Start screen if you're using a tablet PC in tablet mode).

Windows 10 has a new sign in process that allows you to use new ways to access Windows on your device. If your account is the only one on your device and your device doesn't have secure login enabled, you are signed in automatically each time you use your device. Otherwise, you'll need to log in to access your device.

Lock Screen

Whenever you start or wake your device, you'll see a Lock screen. This screen is also displayed when you lock your device. Simply tap or click to go the login screen (or directly to the desktop, if applicable).

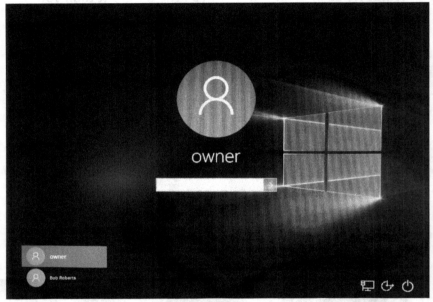

Login Screen

If the device has multiple users, click your account name in the lower left corner of the screen and then provide the required authorization information.

The authorization information required for login can take many forms, but typically includes specifying a:

- Password—A string of upper and lowercase letters, numbers and special characters.
- Pin—A sequence of numbers, usually four or more.
- Picture password—a password drawn on the screen by a series of finger or mouse movements.

If your Windows 10 device has capable hardware, you may also be able to use the following for log in:

- Fingerprint—a touch of your finger to the biometric fingerprint scanner.
- Face scan—a camera on your device can scan your face.

Thus, the basic steps to login are:

1. Tap or click on the Lock screen to access the Login screen.
2. Click your account, if needed.
3. Type your password or PIN.

4. Click the login button ( ).

TIP: Click the **Reveal** ( ) icon to see the password or PIN you typed.

9. Navigating the New Desktop

In Windows 10, Microsoft moved the furniture around and provided new options on the desktop. Most of these new options are available on the taskbar—the bar shown by default at the bottom of the desktop.

The Taskbar

The taskbar has many options. Each option has a specific purpose that will be discussed next. Icons for programs you have open are added to the taskbar automatically. This makes it easier to work with programs. For example, you can use the program icons to switch from one program to another if you have more than one running at a time.

Start Button

You use the Start button to display the Start menu, which in turn allows you to open apps and access features of the operating system.

Search Box with Cortana

The Search box allows you to search for items on your Windows devices or on the web. When Cortana is enabled, the Search box looks as shown above, letting you know you can use your voice to ask Cortana questions. Regardless of whether Cortana is enabled, you can always type text in the Search box to search as well.

Taskbar Icons

The taskbar icons let you use some Windows features with just a tap or a click.

Notification Area

As the name implies, the Notification area is where Windows notifies you about things that are happening on your Windows device. Windows displays notifications for various reasons, including when there are problems or issues you should be aware of.

Time and Date

The taskbar always displays the time and date. If you tap or click the time, you'll see the full calendar for the current month.

TIP: While you are viewing the calendar, click **Date And Time Settings** to view more information about the time and date settings, such as the current time zone.

10. Navigating the New Start

Yes, the Start menu is back in Windows 10 (after being replaced in Windows 8.1). That doesn't mean it's the same Start you may be used to. Start has in fact changed a lot.

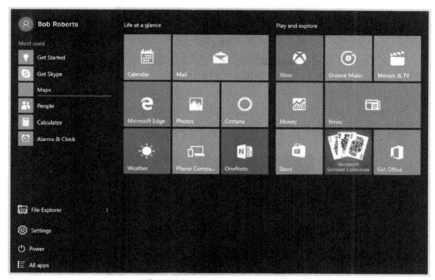

The New Start Menu

Start is divided into two several areas:

- Information and options
- Tiles for apps

Name of Current User

On the left, you have information and options beginning with the name of the currently logged in user. If you click the user name, you can get additional options.

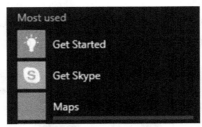

Most Used Apps

Below the user name is a list of the most used apps. Click an app to open it.

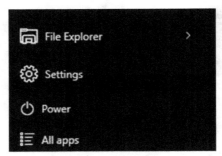

Windows Options

In the lower left corner, you have options that allow you to work with Windows 10:

- File Explorer—Opens the File Explorer, which has replaced Windows Explorer as the go to tool for working with files and folders.
- Settings—Opens the Settings app, which allows you to configure many Windows settings, though Control Panel is still used to configure many other settings.

- Power—Displays power options for managing the power state of your device.
- All Apps—Opens the All Apps view on the Start menu so you can find apps that are installed and available for your use.

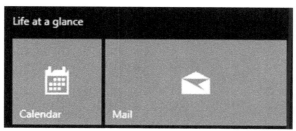

App Tiles

On the right, you have tiles for apps. Tiles replace the traditional program icons used in earlier releases of Windows. Clicking a tile launches the related program.

> **TIP**: Windows 10 has two types of tiles: live tiles and regular tiles. Live tiles display updates and recent information. For example, the tile for the Weather app displays information about current weather without you having to start the app.

11. Navigating the Tablet Screen

If you are using a tablet or small device, such as a smart phone, Windows 10 will automatically use tablet mode. Tablet mode is designed to make it easier to work with touch screens, especially on small devices.

In tablet mode, Windows 10 works different from the way it works in standard mode. When you log in, you see the Tablet screen by default.

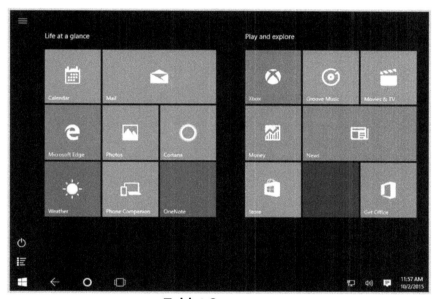

Tablet Screen

The Tablet screen combines features of the Start menu and desktop. As with Start, tiles are displayed and clicking a tile launches the related program.

Menu Button

To get the full Start options, you must click the Menu button, which is in the upper left corner of the screen. You'll then see user information, most used apps, and Windows options.

Back Button

In tablet mode, each app you open is displayed full screen. One way to switch apps is to use the Back button. Click Back to return either to the previous app screen or to the Start screen.

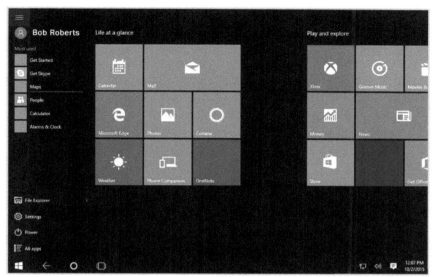

Tablet Screen with Menu Options

As shown in the figure above, the menu options displayed are similar to when you are using Windows 10 with Tablet mode turned off. To hide the additional options, simply click the Menu button again.

Notifications Button

TIP: To turn Tablet mode on or off, click the Notifications button and then click Tablet Mode.

12. Working with Multiple Desktops

Your desktop is where you go to work with your apps. When you open apps, their windows are displayed on the desktop. In earlier releases of Windows, you had a single desktop. Now thanks to the Virtual Desktop System in Windows 10, you can create multiple desktops and easily switch between them.

To add a virtual desktop:

1. Click the **Task View** () button on the taskbar.
2. Click **New Desktop**.

After Windows creates the new desktop, your original desktop is shown as Desktop 1 and the new desktop is shown as Desktop 2. If you create another desktop, that desktop will be shown as Desktop 3, and so on.

TIP: Each virtual desktop is a space where you can open and arrange app windows. At work, you could have one virtual desktop space for each project you are working on. At home, you could have one virtual desktop when you are for working from home and one virtual desktop for when you are relaxing and connecting with friends on social media.

To switch from one desktop to another:

1. Click the **Task View** (![]) button on the taskbar to display a preview of the available desktops.
2. Click the desktop you want to use.

Windows switches to the desktop you selected and displays the windows opened on this desktop. If you start new apps, those apps open on the new desktop.

To close a desktop:

1. Click the **Task View** (![]) button on the taskbar to display a preview of the available desktops.
2. Move the mouse pointer over the desktop you want to close.
3. Click **Close** (![]).

13. Searching Your Computer & the Internet

Plain language search is one of the most important connected features of Windows 10. These built-in search features make it easier to find apps, settings, and documents on your device, as well as websites on the Internet. To use the search feature, all you need to do is enter a question or keyword in the Search box.

Windows provides other ways to search as well, including using File Explorer, Microsoft Edge and Internet Explorer—all of which have their own search boxes. When you search using File Explorer, you search for documents and data files on your device. When you search using a web browser, such as Microsoft Edge, you search websites on the Internet.

To perform a basic search:

1. Click in the Search box and type your question or keywords.

> **TIP**: If the Search box isn't displayed on the taskbar, click **Start** and then type your search text in the Search box.

2. Windows displays the top matches with names that include your search text. The best matches are shown first. Other results are organized by category, such as whether a result is a system setting, in the Windows Store or from a website.
3. Click the item you want and Windows opens the related app, setting, document or website.

If you get too many results or simply can't find the item you are looking for, you may need to modify the search results so that you only see the type of results you are interested in. For example, it may be helpful to only see items from your device or only items from the Web.

To perform an advanced or modified search:

1. Click in the Search box and type your question or keywords.

2. Windows displays the top matches with names that include your search text. If you see the item you want, click it and skip the remaining steps. Otherwise, continue this procedure.

3. To streamline the results, click **My Stuff** to only see results from your device or click **Web** to only see results from the Web.

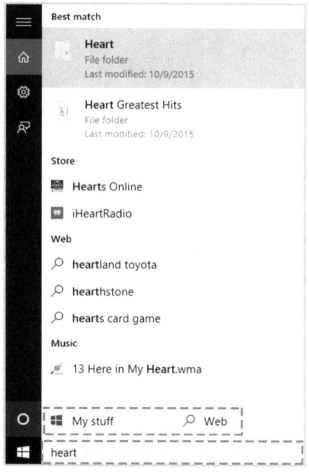

4. By default, results are sorted by Most Relevant. To sort results by Most Recent, click in the **Sort** list and then select **Most Recent**.

5. By default, results of all types are shown. To show only a specific type of result, such as Apps, Settings or Documents, click in the **Show** list and then select the item type.

6. If there are too many similar items, only a subset of the items is shown. Click the **See All** option to display all of the items.

7. Click the item you want and Windows opens the related app, setting, document or website.

14. Syncing Your Settings

If you have more than one device running Windows 10, you can use the same Microsoft account on each device and get the connected benefits I talked about earlier, including access to your universal apps and unified settings. This gives you a consistent working environment across your devices and consistent access to your data.

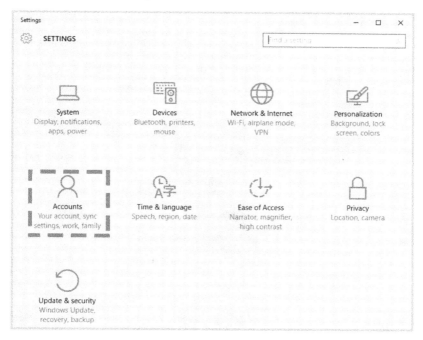

To sync data between your devices:

1. Click **Start** (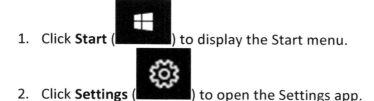) to display the Start menu.

2. Click **Settings** ( ) to open the Settings app.

3. Click **Accounts** to display the Accounts window.
4. Click **Sync Your Settings**.
5. Click the **Sync Settings** switch to **On**.
6. Under Individual Sync Settings, all switches are On by default. Click the switch to **Off** for any setting that you do not want to sync.

> **TIP**: If you toggle sync switches on or off, those changes are applied the next time Windows syncs.

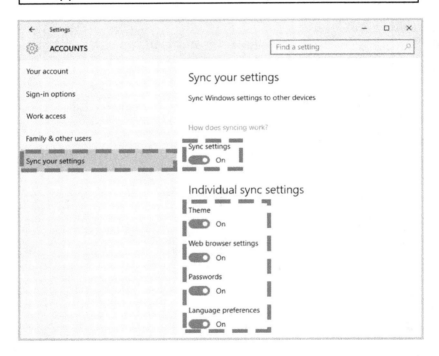

15. Locking Your Screen

When you step away from your computer or put away your device, you may want to lock the screen to prevent others from accessing your device.

To lock your screen:

1. Click **Start** () to display the Start menu.
2. Click your user name at the top of the menu.

Change account settings

Lock

Sign out

Bob Roberts
Signed in

owner

3. Click **Lock**.

TIP: You can also lock your screen by pressing the

Windows logo key (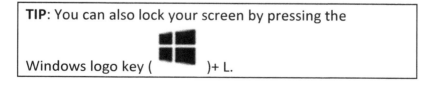)+ L.

You can also configure your device to automatically turn off the screen after it has been idle for a specified amount of time. To configure the screen to turn off automatically:

1. Click **Start** (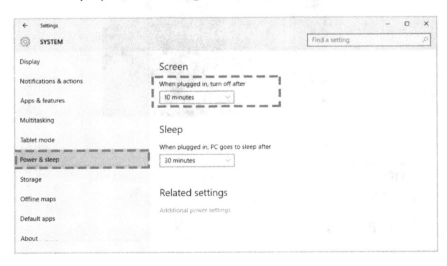) to display the Start menu.

2. Click **Settings** ( ) to open the Settings app.

3. Click **System**, then click **Power & Sleep**.

4. Under **Screen**, use the **When Plugged In, Turn Off After** list to specify the number of minutes of idle time before Windows turns off the display when running on A/C power.

5. If available, use the **On Battery, Turn Off After** list under the **Screen** heading to specify the number of minutes of idle time before Windows turns off the display when running on battery power.

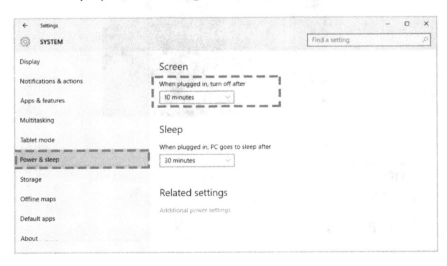

16. Connecting to Networks

If your device has built-in wireless networking, you can connect to a wireless access point to access wireless networks. Connecting to a network allows you to access any resources hosted on the network. If the wireless access point also is connected to the Internet, then connecting to the wireless network allows your device to access the Internet.

There are two general types of wireless networks:

- Open
- Secured

Open networks, often listed as Guest networks when you visit a coffee shop or other retailer, typically don't require you to use a security key or password. They do, however, generally require you to accept service terms and sign in.

In contrast, secured networks require you to have a security key or password to access the network. They may also require you to accept service terms and sign in.

To connect to an open wireless network:

1. Click **Network** ( ) to display the Network sidebar.
2. Click the network that you want to connect to.
3. To have Windows connect automatically in the future, click **Connect Automatically**. The related checkbox will then have a checkmark.
4. Click **Connect**.

5. Wait a few seconds. If sign-in is required, Windows should prompt you. Click **Yes**.
6. Windows opens a browser window. If prompted, accept the terms of service, and then click the option provided for connecting to the network. Otherwise, simply click the option provided for connecting.

TIP: Sometimes the option for accepting the terms of service is a tiny checkbox that's hardly visible. Here, do your best to tap or click in the checkbox. When selected, the box will have a checkmark inside it.

To connect to a secured wireless network or an open network with a password:

1. Click **Network** ( ) to display the Network sidebar.
2. Click the network that you want to connect to.
3. To have Windows connect automatically in the future, click **Connect Automatically**. The related checkbox will then have a checkmark.
4. Click **Connect**.
5. Enter the security key or password when prompted. If

needed, click and hold the reveal button ( ) to temporarily display the characters you entered.
6. Click **Next**.

Windows may prompt you to confirm whether it can locate other computers or devices on the network. If you are on your home network, click **Yes**. Otherwise, click **No**.

If additional sign-in is required or acceptance of service terms is required, Windows may also prompt you. Click **Yes**. If prompted, accept the terms of service, and then click the option provided for connecting or agreeing. Otherwise, simply click the option provided for connecting or agreeing.

> **TIP**: Sometimes when sign in is required, Windows won't open a browser window with the additional options needed for sign in. If this happens, click **Microsoft Edge** (
>
>
>) on the taskbar and then enter a web address in the browser window or simply try to browse to a web address, such as www.yahoo.com. This should force Windows to open the sign-in page.

If you don't want Windows to be connected to a network any more, you can disconnect from the network:

1. Click **Network** () to display the Network sidebar.
2. Click the network to which you are connected.
3. Click **Disconnect** to disconnect from the wireless network.

17. Switching Users

If you want to save your workspace, you can switch users instead of signing out. When you switch users, Windows keeps a snapshot of all your open windows and documents and allows you to resume your work next time you log in.

To switch users:

1. Click **Start** ( ) to display the Start menu.
2. Click your user name at the top of the menu.

Change account settings

Lock

Sign out

Bob Roberts
Signed in

owner

3. Click the account of the user you are switching to.
4. This user can then login and begin working.

TIP: Before switching users, make sure you save your documents and other work. This way your work will be preserved if the other user needs to shut down or restart the device.

18. Signing Out

If you share your device with other users, you may want to sign out when you are done using Windows. When you sign out, Windows closes all the open apps and frees the memory and other resources the apps were using. Because of this, you should always save your work before you sign out. Once you've signed out, a different user can then sign in.

To sign out:

1. Click **Start** () to display the Start menu.
2. Click your user name at the top of the menu.

3. Click **Sign Out**.

Windows tries to sign you out quickly. Any apps that don't respond immediately to the close request are flagged and you may see a prompt concerning whether you want to force close the apps. If you wait just a few moments, the apps should close normally and be removed from the Force Close prompt. Allowing apps to close normally ensures Windows can perform any necessary background tasks, including saving your progress and work.

If you don't want to or can't wait, you can allow Windows to force close apps. This is sometimes necessary for apps that have become unresponsive. However, keep in mind that this may result it lost progress or work when you sign in to your account later.

Lessons in Review

Thank you...

Thank you for purchasing **Windows 10 Jump Start**. Please support this book if you found it to be useful. I hope to write other books and your support will help me do that!

Notes

Notes